This book belongs to:

WANNA SMOKE?
YEAH, ALPACA BOWL

MARIGUANA

LLAMA ROLL
ONE MORE

GREENRILLA

PUFF PUFF
PANDA

LIFE IS
GOOD

I'm Damn Fried

STONED

Pass it

Octopot

Wow this wasn't Grass

KEEP IT
GREEN

INHALE
THE GOOD
SHIT
EXHALE
THE BAD SHIT

GOOD VIBES

MY MANTRA:
RISE&GRIND

HIPPIE-CORN

WHERE THERE'S
WEED
THERE'S HOPE

Made in the USA
Las Vegas, NV
04 December 2024

13332218R10031